About the Author

Angela Hudson grew up in Monroe, Washington. Angela has loved writing poetry since she was a little girl. She found it to be a great way to express herself. Angela has battled cancer since 2018, which brought her closer to God, inspiring her to write again. Angela is happily married to the love of her life, Larry Hudson. They live a quiet and happy life in Eastern Washington.

Perfect Timing

Angela Hudson

Perfect Timing

Olympia Publishers
London

www.olympiapublishers.com
OLYMPIA PAPERBACK EDITION

Copyright © Angela Hudson 2024

The right of Angela Hudson to be identified as author of
this work has been asserted in accordance with sections 77 and 78 of
the Copyright, Designs and Patents Act 1988.

All Rights Reserved

No reproduction, copy or transmission of this publication
may be made without written permission.
No paragraph of this publication may be reproduced,
copied or transmitted save with the written permission of the publisher,
or in accordance with the provisions
of the Copyright Act 1956 (as amended).

Any person who commits any unauthorised act in relation to
this publication may be liable to criminal
prosecution and civil claims for damage.

A CIP catalogue record for this title is
available from the British Library.

ISBN: 978-1-83543-122-1

First Published in 2024

Olympia Publishers
Tallis House
2 Tallis Street
London
EC4Y 0AB

Printed in Great Britain

Dedication

I would like to dedicate this book to my husband, parents, sister, nephews, and nieces. Thank you for being my biggest fans.

Acknowledgment

I would like to thank my husband, Larry, for his input and encouragement while I wrote this book.

ADAM AND EVE

From the dust, Adam was created
Dominion over everything he was fated
Giving names unto the animals he did this all alone
Then God gave him Eve from his sleeping rib bone
Together in Eden they were without guilt and shame
Until Eve bit an apple and a snake was to blame
Now they were cast out with covers on their skin
Forever working the earth because of their sin
The original parents were Adam and Eve
May we learn from their mistakes
For only God we should believe.

BALD EAGLE

The mighty bird takes his rest
The bald eagle upon his nest
Surveying all of his domain
This bird is one hundred percent American
He eyes his next meal, flying in with stealth
The squeal of a field mouse is his dinner bell
The claws on his talons are sharp as blades
Securely gripping his reluctant prey
His six-foot wingspan is a sight to behold
Majestic in flight, his strength is bold
As like our nation, his beauty is fierce
Independent and strong, we will all persevere.

BALLERINA

My little ballerina, you are a beautiful child of light
Full of creativity with a smile so bright
You are God's creation; you are perfectly made
A beautiful work of art that will never fade
Your laughter is contagious, you give us all a big grin
Always chase rainbows for their beauty has no end
Hold onto God's love, He will help you to fly
Beautiful ballerina, you can dance across the sky
My sweet girl, how you love to sing
Your voice is like a butterfly as it spreads its wings
As you go through life, remember this, my dear
You are never alone, God is always near.

BAPTISM

To be born again, you need living water
Being cleansed of your sins by our Heavenly Father
You are dressed all in white, a beautiful attire
Being made new, baptized in fire
The Holy Ghost is a gift you receive on this day
He will guide your heart, He will lead the way
With your fresh baptism, you are made whole
God has now cleansed you, embrace your new soul.

BASIC TRAINING

What an adventure to be a recruit
Dropping for push-ups and learning to salute
Wearing a uniform at Dress Right Dress
Eating in a chow hall or maybe the Mess
Rising in the morning well before dawn
Standing in formation on the front lawn
The adventure of new people and seeing a new place
Would be more fun without a drill instructor in your face
Marching through the mud, you're covered from helmet to boot
Heading to the rifle range learning how to shoot
Basic training is now over, you graduate today
You're officially a soldier representing the USA.

BEACH

Lying on the beach, my body on the sand
A strawberry margarita in my hand
The waves are rolling
As the sea breeze is blowing
I hear the coconuts clink as the palm trees sway
Being sun-kissed by the warm sunny day
My mind is empty except for one notion
I just want to be covered in sun tan lotion
The tide is beginning to rise and crash against the rocks
The seagulls take to flight, I can hear them squawk
The lighthouse siren is getting really loud, "No, wait!"
That's my alarm clock, I have to go to work now.

BEAUTY WITHIN

Her daily struggle is not how she feels,
Because the look on the outside to her is what's real
Always at the parlor, afraid of what others see
Her makeup, her dress, does she look pretty?
The mirror is her enemy, very rarely her friend
Not content with what she sees from beginning to end
Her size may not be perfect, but her kind heart is
She is perfectly created by an image that is His
She is truly beautiful inside and out
For the beauty within is what it's about.

BLUE

Here's to those who wear the blue
So forever grateful for what you do
When in your uniform, hold your head high
Be proud of yourself and the thin blue line
You are here for a reason to serve and protect
Wear your badge with honor, you deserve respect
You keep people safe, that's your ultimate goal
Be careful, brothers and sisters, when out on patrol.

BRIGHTER

For every angel made of snow
There is a smile with an outward glow
For every decoration that has a sparkle and shine
They are even brighter on a tree of pine
For every river that is wild and fast
There is a bridge that will allow us to pass
For every story that has never been told
There is a rainbow with a pot of gold
For every thought we have in a dream
There is an action with a sight unseen
For every star that lights up the sky
There is a peace watching life go by.

CALM

Breathing in a moment and taking it all in
Calming my surroundings and my thoughts within
Enjoying every second of my peaceful quiet
Embracing the silence when I can find it
My favorite book, it is within my reach
Soaking up the pages as if it were the sun on the beach
In my moving world, I am happy to be still
The calmness of my day leaves me content and fulfilled.

CATERPILLAR

Admire the caterpillar who walks on many legs
Working together as a unit with each individual peg
He loves to bite on an apple or an occasional leaf
With his time as a caterpillar so very brief
He will soon wrap himself in a giant cocoon
He will wait to be beautiful; he will be there soon
Weeks have now passed, he no longer hides
Look at that butterfly as he takes to the sky.

CHRISTMAS CARD

Christmas is upon us like the fallen snow
With this card, we want to let you know
We have been truly blessed by God, family, and friends
May happiness and joy fill your season without end
Merry Christmas to all far and near
May God bless you in the new year.

CREATED

When God created the ocean and the creatures within
They were made only for water for they can only swim
Removing them from the water, they would surely die
For they are not birds made to fly among the sky
When God created plants, they are to live within the dirt
Spreading far and wide below the ground within the earth
Removing them from dirt, they would surely die
For they are not animals who live wildly outside
When God created man, He took us from Himself
Made in His image like nothing else
Removing us from God, we will surely die
For God is the only one that brings eternal life
Everything that is created comes from God above
When God created earth, He created us with love.

DANNIE

I once had a friend whom I found to be quite witty
He always had a joke; some were good, some were naughty
He was a big man with a heart even bigger
We enjoyed our cowboy shoots and had fun pulling the trigger
He was a life member of the Elk Foundation
A generous man who gave heartfelt donations
He lived for going hunting and playing practical jokes
Then sitting around the campfire telling stories to folks
He was a very vocal man, his opinion he often shared
His honesty was sometimes brutal, but yet I found him to be fair
He would call me every week and we would talk on the phone
We would discuss our day and our love for Yellowstone
How I miss my friend, a great man was he
I will always remember him fondly, my buddy Dannie.

ETERNAL AND FOREVER

Heavenly Father, you are the light and the truth
We are forever nothing unless we have you
Your Son took upon himself the sin of all men
Through your graceful forgiveness, we are alive again
You are pure love of which cannot be measured
You are the God of everything, the one true Creator
Our life is but a blink on earth we do treasure
Only with you God we can live eternal and forever.

FAKE

Beware of the people that smile to your face
When you turn around, all they do is disgrace
They speak words of kindness with what you want to hear
The words they are saying are lies to the ear
They hide as your friends, family, or other
Posing to love you as Cain to his brother
You must keep your eyes open to see beneath the mask
Discern good from evil and stand steadfast.

FATHER

I give all thanks unto thy Father
He is my shield and my protector
His command of love is easy to follow
His loving embrace erases my sorrow
He removes all my fears, dries up my tears
His words of inspiration are comfort to my ear
The smile on his face shows me God's Grace
Forever in his Glory is my eternal place.

FEAR

Fear is not of God do not let it in
For it will cripple and paralyze deep down from within
Fear is the gateway to everything bad
Fear will take away all that you have
Creating paranoia is what fear does best
Shaking you to your core, never letting you rest
When it comes to sin, fear is the first
God tells us to trust in Him when our fear is at our worst
Faith over fear is a peaceful cure
Do not be afraid for with God, you will endure.

FISHING

Getting up early because I can't wait
I grab my pole and fishing bait
I jump in my boat and pull up anchor
Wanting to catch fish both now and later
I cast off the bow, it hits with a splash
I just got a bite, the fish bit fast
My pole is bent, arched into a curve
It is hard to reel as the fish continues to swerve
As the fish gets closer, I reach for the net
Trying not to fall with everything slippery and wet
The fish is at the boat; he is bigger than I thought
And with a quick release, my line he no longer fought.

FUR BALL

A tiny little fur ball known as my pet
He is nothing but attitude and does not let me forget
His claws are sharp and his whiskers are long
When I try to sleep, he meows his nightly song
He likes to have his tummy rubbed, but only when he sees fit
If he doesn't want me to, I will definitely get bit
He loves to lie on blankets and especially on my lap
He expects me not to move while he is taking his nap
My pet has a personality, this I can't ignore
If wasn't for my fur ball, life would be a bore.

GIFT

The gift of prayer is a blessing God has bestowed upon me
The ability to speak with Him as He listens lovingly
I bow my head in service as I raise my hands to Him
Feeling His Holy Spirit and the grace within
My prayer is but a question that He can only answer
For kneeling down before Him, my life I must surrender.

GOOD FIGHT

Make faith your good fight
Use it to empower with all your might
Be strong, steadfast
Let God's presence help you at last
Take a scripture and read it aloud
Let everyone hear it, stand up and be proud
Fighting the good fight will bring both joy and pain
Do not fear death for you will live again
No need to back down when enemies are at your door
They will soon find out what God has in store.

HUNTING

I am up early ready to go
All dressed in my cammo
I have my rifle and sharp knife
This is what I love most in life
The light is on the horizon, yet still dark
Hoping my shot will hit the mark
Sitting in my blind with the chill in the air
Fingers are numb, I can't feel my derriere
Nothing is moving they're awful aloof
I haven't even heard the sound of a hoof
Sitting in anticipation, my stomach starts to grind
You would not believe the noises coming from this blind
Hours go by, my target is here
A large buck, one heck of a deer
I load my rifle and take aim
Click goes the gun, it has jammed again!
As I do the walk of shame to my truck all alone
The only thing I shot today were the pics on my phone.

JONAH

Jonah was a Hebrew who feared the Lord
But he wanted to run and hide and be sought after no more
He fled to a ship; upon the ocean he did sleep
Until a storm came upon him with waves so steep
To ensure the calmness of the sea
The sailors threw Jonah into the waters so deep
With great fear and a final wish
Jonah was swallowed by a giant fish
For three days and three nights, the waves were plenty
There he prayed deep within the belly
He thanked the Lord for freedom from the pit
Then out onto land from the fish he was spit
With Thanksgiving, Jonah thanked the Lord
He will no longer hide from God anymore.

KISSES FROM HEAVEN

When we are children, we love a kiss from Mom
She heals all our wounds and makes bad things begone
As a child of God, you need His kiss too
Kisses from Heaven are His gift to you
A kiss is a sign of caring, it is a sign of love
When you say a prayer, a kiss returns to God above.

LAYLA

There is a hole in my heart as of this day
I said goodbye to my friend as they passed away
Every day by my side, year after year
I miss you being near me, how I want you here
Your everyday greeting made my day shine
When we were together, I knew all was fine
You were more than just a dog, you were my world
I will miss you, my Layla, my beautiful baby girl.

LIFE

When times are hard and cut like a knife
Open the bible and know God's word is life
He will take your pain and remove it ten-fold
He has you forever; it is you He will hold
Hear his words, speak the truth
His love is true when He speaks to you
Whenever you doubt or question your path
God has the answer, you just have to ask.

LITTLE ONE

My precious little one, this is a special day
You are truly loved in every single way
God has brought you to us as a gift from above
For you, little one, make us happy and full of love
Your smile is as sunshine; it brightens up a room
You make our lives complete; we love you to the moon.

MORNING SON

The morning Son has risen
The third day, all is forgiven
Across the sky, His Glory does shine
His loving warmth forever divine
The sky does kneel to the Son's embrace
Waking up to Him brings peace to this place.

NEPHEWS

My nephews are boys who are strong and kind
They love with all their heart and their personalities uniquely shine
The oldest loves his country whether it's music or where he lives
He dreams of being an officer with a badge that's only his
The one who is next can paint a work of art
And in the game of lacrosse, he is truly set apart
When it comes to sports, the third one gives his all
He can tackle the best of them; he is number one in football
The youngest one has a mind for financial success
A young entrepreneur, he will run his own business
They are close brothers and ever so tall
But beware of little sister, she rules them all.

NIGHT SHIFT

The sun is now down; it's officially dark
My night shift has started, working another graveyard
The city is asleep while I try to stay awake
Eagerly awaiting my first coffee break
The office is quiet with just a skeleton crew
Trying to keep busy with not much to do
I sleep during the day with the incoming sun
Trying to keep my eyes closed, easier said than done
Night shifts are needed though they are hard
I am ready for the day when I can sleep in the dark.

NO VACANCY

Traveling cross country with miles behind
Needing to rest, relax and unwind
I stop at every exit to look for a room
Signs say "no vacancy," is this really true?
Further on I go to travel once again
Requiring a hotel or a bed and breakfast inn
The road is getting longer as my mind starts to ponder
Are there any vacancies? I'm beginning to wonder
My eyes are getting heavy and my backside is numb
I'm ready to call it a night, I'm ready to be done
Wanting to give up, I give it one more try
I see a vacancy; it lights up the sky
I've checked into the hotel, ready to count sheep
As my luck would go… "I Can't Sleep!"

OPPOSITE

How tall you are, slim and petite
I am short with a round physique
You love it hot with the sun shining bright
I love it cold with the ground all white
You like it quiet and away from a crowd
I love the attention and enjoy being loud
You enjoy eating healthy, veggies are your thing
I'll have a pizza topped with everything
How we are so opposite, this we can't deny
But opposites attract especially for a girl and a guy.

PERFECT TIMING

Wondering why, when, and where
Asking ourselves are we going to get there
Frustration sets in, it's not happening fast
We want to be in the future and out of the past
Always in a hurry, never taking a pause
Coming to the realization it is not our time, it is God's
He moves us forward as He sees fit
Without a mistake, God's timing is perfect.

QUESTIONING

How far will you go to serve the Lord our God with your heart and soul?
Would you risk your life and walk through fire
While ridding yourself of your sinful desires?
Would you shy away from foolish delight
To fill yourself up with His inner light?
To prove you are of God's flock
Would you stand to be ridiculed, harassed, and mocked?
To learn God's word and let Him light the way
Would you abandon all your knowledge and what you know today?
To get your questions answered, it is God you must seek, but ask yourself this question…
How strong is my belief?

RAINSTORM

The clouds have grown dark with thunderous sound
I can smell the rain as it floats to the ground
The temperature of the air has changed its degree
I can see the lightning as it tries to catch a tree
The wind has now decided it wants to play
Grabbing what it can and sending it astray
The lakes are rising as the rivers are running
I can only hope there will be no flooding
The lights begin to flash as candles are being lit
It will be a long night in front of my radio I do sit
How I love a rainstorm, exciting as they may be
I'm ready for the morning, but it was sure fun for me.

RED SEA

Atop the cloud, He leads the way
As of fire, He turns night into day
Leading His children to be forever free
Crossing the division of the Red Sea
The water does rise as to a wall on both sides
Led by a staff raised to the sky
Coming from behind, chariots do follow
Leading their army is a hard-hearted Pharoah
Upon dry land, His children fled to shore
While watching the Pharoah sink to the ocean floor.

ROAD TRIP

A road trip is miles that takes us away
Far from the stresses of the everyday
A road map before us, our destination is clear
Excited to see what lies ahead, forgetting everything else in the rear-view mirror
Taking turns driving while the other sleeps
Filling the tank again, this bill is not cheap
We are seeing new states, each different from the last
Some have mountains, others just grass
Our car is full of food, clothes, and junk
There isn't even room inside our trunk
Restaurants are the kitchen while hotels become our home
Living life as nomads on the road we do roam
When we feel a vacation calling and want to leave today
We simply take a road trip and the miles carry us away.

ROOT

Through the root that is deep buried into the ground
You can feel the life growing all around
The branches grow straight, wide, and tall
Reaching for the heavens, creating shade for us all
The leaves grow green as they stretch far and wide
Providing a home down low and on high
It sways with the breeze, yet sturdy and strong
You can count the rings, its life is very long
The tree maybe a forest or the forest a tree
But without the root, it could never be.

SEASON ANEW

The rain on the porch, the wind in the air
The birds fly by without a care
The temperature falling with a season anew
Out goes the heat, bringing in the cool
The leaves are now changing, no colors of green
Oranges and brown are now what is seen
The animals scurry to store up their food
While I cook a pot of hot venison stew
A fire is lit, under a blanket I lay
The animals and I are ready to hibernate.

SCHOOL

Reading, writing, arithmetic
I do not like school, it makes me sick
Always having homework and having to take tests
I don't want to be in class and have to do my best
Why must I learn, I don't feel the need
Why must I go to school, why must I read
For here is the answer you have to teach yourself
Without an education, there is no future and no wealth
We are learning constantly, it begins at birth
Life is its own school, it teaches while on earth
So, buckle down in class and improve that grade
Once you receive your diploma, you will have it made.

SHARE

Among the air, the Word we must share
From nation to nation, everywhere
For us He is calling, His time is at hand
We must spread His message to all the land
He will come with the thunder, so full of Grace
Near and afar He will take his place
For us to be saved and to be made whole
We need Jesus Christ to save our soul.

SINAI

On the mountain, Sinai be its name
God came down as smoke and flame
The sky grew dark with thunder and sound
While music of trumpets played all around
People gathered near the mountain, but knew not to touch
They needed to just listen so God could teach them much
Atop of this mountain, Moses took a stand
Holding God's commandments, five in each hand
For these are God's words and rules to live by
Be thankful for the tablets that were brought to Sinai.

SING

Praise the Lord with dance and song
May all rejoice and sing along
Sing His praise with a joyful noise
Raise your hands let Him hear your voice
Sing hallelujah in all you do
Feel God's Grace wash over you.

SNOW

Six feet of snow and twenty below
Winter is here, it's on the go
Snowflakes are falling, they are stacking high
I hold out my tongue to give one a try
I pull down my beanie and tighten my gloves
I'm going to move this giant snowball with one big shove
I just made a snowman that can touch the sky
With a carrot and some coal, he has a face to say "Hi"
Eager to go sledding, I must find a hill
Flying down fast is the ultimate thrill
The snow has now stopped, off to the house I go
Time to warm up with a cup of hot cocoa.

SOUL MATE

Life was so empty without you and will be again if you leave
I can't bear the heartache of you not being with me
I now know true happiness as I never have before
If you go away, I will know love, no more
The moment I saw your face, my smile has never erased
It is with you forever, I do long to place
With your eyes of blue and a warm heart so true
I want to forever lie down next to you
What I can read in your silence says more than your words
With the holding of my hand, I hear every word
I do believe in fate and that it always has its way
I know deep down it's true, for it is your name that I take.

STONES

Out of Egypt, they did flee
To the land of milk and honey
From every man of every tribe
A basket of fruit to give as tithe
Collecting the stones to whitewash with lime
Keeping His Commandments one plus nine
With the parting of the sea
They now thank God who set them free.

STORM

I feel it now, the incoming storm
Bracing myself trying to keep warm
The lights are all flickering
The wind is at the door
I have no idea what lies in store
My mind begins to race as the windows start to shake
Saying to myself, "I hope they don't break"
The rain is getting louder, it is stampeding on the roof
Sounds more like hail, but I don't want to look
The sirens are in the distance telling people not to fear
Help is on the way, it is almost here
The storm has now passed, there is much to do
For we will rebuild, because that is what we do.

TEDDY BEAR

Funny, furry, and fuzzy my teddy bear is
He has lots of hugs that he loves to give
Teddy brings me comfort when we sit and cuddle
Though we have more fun when we jump into a puddle
We go everywhere together, especially on trips
And when I have some milk, he always gets a sip
Teddy loves TV and watches it with me
Then we play around the house, a game of Hide-N-Go Seek
When I get tired, my teddy bear is the best
We fall asleep together and get a good night's rest.

THE ONE

Seek the One who does ride among the cloud
Praise His name, Praise aloud
Feel His Grace as it flows from the Son
Watching the wickedness be undone
Share in His Glory by reading His word
Spread His message, let Him be heard
The light of truth will shine brightly through you
When you let God guide you in all that you do.

THREE

Three years have gone by, it is that time again
For my third surgery, the cancer has set in
I try to be positive and ask for lots of prayer
I thought it was over, but it was hiding there
It crept ever so slowly going undetected
Causing the body to secretly be infected
My attitude is good and my will is very strong
God made me a fighter for recovery is long
I'm once again tested, but keeping the faith
For when this is over, God's plan is in place
Third time is a charm most people say
I know this to be true, for Jesus arose the third day.

WATERS

Dear Heavenly Father
Only you can cross these waters
No matter the weather or the waves
You are the path that lights the way
Though times may be turbulent and ever so rough
You keep the waters calm for you are enough
You speak as of water your voice a tidal wave
It is through your grace that we are forever saved.

WELL

There is a story I'd like to tell
It is of a woman who visited a well
She came upon a man asking for a drink
Did He just talk to me? she did think
For she was an outcast among his kind
Little did she know, she was the one He wanted to find
She felt so embarrassed because of her past
The woman did not know she was saved at last
He was the Christ; to her, His story He did tell
She received the living water, no longer needing the well.

WRITER

They say to make a living you must earn a decent wage
Why can't I make a living putting words to a page
My memories of the past and the future are so clear
For with the words I write, I bring them both near
I try to paint a picture one word at a time
Creating a new memory with every single line
My pen is as a paintbrush writing a masterpiece
For every completed book it is a canvas that speaks.

YOU

You created my story from beginning to end
Always at my side my eternal friend
You know my thoughts before I even think
Keeping me calm when I am on the brink
A path is laid before me, only You know the Way
Keeping me on track when I go astray
My tongue is sometimes fire, speaking words that burn
My ears often go quiet not hearing what I must learn
You try to teach me humility to my conscience you do speak
Reminding me of Your forgiveness and it is You I must seek.

Printed in the USA
CPSIA information can be obtained
at www.ICGtesting.com
LVHW090014301024
795097LV00003B/393

9 781835 431221